Self-help guide for second-age couple formation

BY

JOHN SPECIAL

Self-help guide for second-age couple formation

Why are there so many separations and divorces in the world?

Why are there so many lonely older people looking for a partner and trying to rebuild their lives?

When I decided to write this self-help guide, I did so for basically two reasons. The first, when looking at the statistics on the number of divorces and separations that occur annually, and the number of older men and women, who are looking for partners on dating apps and social networks trying to rebuild their lives. And the second, when looking many of my friends in couples, which I considered as examples of perfect couples, separated after a few years. Then I decided to try to capture in a text, a small contribution that would serve as a guide for all those people who feel lonely, to find someone to share their life with, and most importantly, give some tips to stay together until the end of their days.

This book is not an extensive manual, where the topics that are treated are developed in depth, but it is a summary of how to approach a relationship and maintain it.

We all know what love is, how to conquer a person and keep them by our side, but it is also true that once we secure the bond, we let ourselves be, we forget to work on our relationship with the person we love, and so we fall into mistakes that can cost us a separation or estrangement from our spouse.

It is true that there are no magic formulas or general rules for a successful relationship, but there are certain elements or factors that can make a relationship more harmonious, bearable and lasting for both members of a couple.

However, every day more and more people are breaking their ties and drifting apart, and this is happening in all cultures and with people of all ages Thousands of books have been written about the causes of relationship problems, as well as how to deal with them.

This book is not intended for young people, who have a lifetime ahead of them to change partners over and over again because they can't find the right person, with very different goals from those of adults, but for those older people who no longer have all the time in the world to find someone to share the rest of their lives with.

It could also be very useful for people who are in a couple, to remember some things that they may have forgotten.

Nowadays, relationships are so accelerated due to the pace of life we lead, where wasting a few seconds is considered a great waste of time, and everything we want, we want it instantly.

Relationships today are no longer like they were 30, 40 or 50 years ago, where two people met, fell in love, had sex, and after a time of knowing each other, which could be short or long, they lived together.

Today, young and old, they have sex before they meet, and agree to live together without knowing anything about each other.

We know that an important aspect for a good relationship is communication, it is a key element in the couple, but it is also true that it is one of the first things that breaks down after a few years or even months after two people have started a new life together.

Another aspect to take into account when starting a relationship, is to get to know the other person. And when we say "getting to know", we mean getting to know that new partner in depth. Not superficially as it happens today, where young people meet, and in a few days they have fallen in love, they have loved each other and they have loved and loved each other.

They say with total conviction, "I LOVE YOU", knowing that in order to love a person you must have gone through many situations together, often difficult, and with time you reach that much desired feeling.

There is a saying: "Marriage is a journey into the unknown, where both must face not only what they do not know about the other person, but also what they do not know about themselves".

That is why it is important to take some time, even if it is not much, to try to get to know ourselves a little bit first before getting to know other people well.

How to know oneself?

You can ask yourself and answer as honestly as possible to questions such as.

What are my strengths and weaknesses?

What are the things I am afraid of?

What are my short, medium and long term goals in my life?

What things am I proud of/a in my life?

What do I regret?

Am I happy or not?

Do I have good self-esteem?

Am I a faithful or unfaithful person?

What is my favorite book, music and movie?

Would I like to go and live in another city or another country? Would I really want to?

What kind of pet do I like?

What things bother me about other people?

What things bother me that other people do to me?

What things bother me about myself?

Perhaps by answering these questions as honestly as possible, you will get to know yourself a little better, and be prepared to get to know other people better, and these same questions could help you get to know other men and women better.

But don't worry too much about this. It's been proven that most people in the world don't know themselves. And it's the same in almost all relationships.

They fall in love and start a life together with someone they barely know externally, only what their eyes see, without getting to know the person in depth, which in the end is the most important thing for a lasting relationship.

Even after years of living together, you don't get to know the person next to you.

Then they leave everything to chance, and if the relationship turns out to be successful, go ahead. If it's a failure, they put up with it or change partners.

That is why it is very important to get to know the loved one as well as possible before taking the transcendental step of living with him or her, because at the beginning of a relationship everything is wonderful. There is nothing that bothers us about the other person.

Even the things that have always bothered us, we omit them, so as not to make our new partner angry, and once we are living together, we do not let them go unnoticed without first getting upset or with reactions that at the beginning we would never have thought of having, and the sum of repeating those things that bother us, in the end make the love bond break.

By not knowing the other person well, you are less likely to have a long lasting relationship.

Today it has become normal for young people to live together shortly after meeting, have children, and after a period of time that is usually short, separate.

This may not occur frequently in first world countries, because of the education they have had, but in second and third world countries it occurs much more frequently.

So let's see what are some of the factors or ingredients that must be taken into account to be successful in this enterprise called marriage or cohabitation.

Love, jealousy, infidelity, bad temper, disinterest, routine, sex, health, health, trust, respect, admiration, empathy, money, good communication, secrets, time, resentment, lies, are some of the aspects to take into account in a relationship. They are many, and not easy to achieve.

Did someone say it was easy to get along well with your loved one?

Not at all, it is one of the most difficult things in life, and to be successful, we must dedicate a lot of time and understanding to our relationship, which is not available to young couples, who live a very accelerated life, dedicating a lot of time to work, business, cars, fun with friends, sports, children, and in the end, to the couple.

And although this does not happen all the time, because there are always exceptions, there are too many cases in which it does. But we who are adults, and who have already given up many of these activities that young people do, do have more time to dedicate to our partner.

One of the words we have already seen, and we will continue to see several times in this text, is RELATIONSHIP, another will be COUPLE. These are key words, which we are going to use a lot.

But let's go back to the beginning, to what we are really interested in at the moment. And answer the question. If I am a single adult, male or female.

How do I meet and win over a person with whom I would like to rebuild my love life?

But before we go to conquer a person, we must prepare our weapons. Do soldiers go to war without weapons and equipment?

We must also prepare our equipment and weapons, but how?

To begin with, taking care of our health. We are the most important thing in our lives, and good health comes first. So a visit to the doctor and a check-up of our organism will do us a lot of good and will save us a lot of headaches in the near future. Nowadays, young people and adults should have a medical check-up regularly, at least once a year. Of course, all these recommendations are not compulsory, but only for those who think it is convenient and have the necessary means to do them, but it does not mean that if you do not do them you will fail.

Another important aspect is to visit the dentist, also if possible, at least once a year, which will make us have a nice smile in front of other people.

I hear a very common phrase from people.

"The most important thing in life is our children," is partly true. But if we are unwell, who will take care of them? We are very important, and we should be in very good health, so that when our loved ones need us, we can be well for them. And by taking care of our body, we will take an important step towards that.

Any other important aspects?

Yes, if we can and we are able, after a medical inspection, to go to a gym. Nowadays it is common to see young people in their twenties training there with adults in their fifties, sixties, seventies or even older, be they men or women.

And if you do not like these facilities, there is no better workout than a good walk, alone or in groups in a square or a park, and dedicate a few hours daily to this healthy outdoor exercise.

Swimming is another sport recommended by physicians for adults.

The difference with the gym is that exercises with a little weight will re-strengthen our muscles and bones, reduce stress, rejuvenate our skin, improve our sleep, better control our weight and heart health, and improve our appearance.

The great thing is to see women and men, older adults training alongside teenagers and young adults.

We must remember that life expectancy today is more than eighty years, and that people who take care of their health, their diet, dedicate time to sports, and complement that with an elegant way of dressing, appear to be between ten to fifteen years younger, there are even people in their seventies who appear to have a maximum of fifty years. Why can't we also be like that?

Today, thanks to scientific advances, biological age is more important than chronological age. Chronological age is just a number, what is important is how we feel.

We can be 30 years old and feel tired and aged like a 70 year old, or conversely, be 70 years old and look and feel like a 50 year old for example.

While our physical health is good, we should not neglect our mental health. It is not for nothing that many famous doctors say that many serious illnesses begin in the mind. A visit to a psychologist will always do us good if we can do it.

You can learn to be a person with a positive attitude by reading books or watching videos on these topics. Have you ever seen the movie "The Secret, The Law of Attraction", if you haven't, it's time to take a look at it. You will come out mentally strengthened even if you are not completely convinced by the messages taught in that one hour long video.

People like to find positive people who motivate them to bring out the best in themselves. We can learn to be frankly positive, becoming that kind of people to help others and motivate them to be better. We will gain good friendships.

HOW DO I GET TO KNOW A PERSON AND GO ON A DATE?

Now let's see, if we are single and assuming we don't know anyone we think is special for a relationship.

How can we get to know a person with whom we can exchange messages at the beginning, and then talk and propose a meeting for a first date?

Nowadays, the ways of meeting people have changed a lot.

They no longer happen as they did thirty and more years ago, where you could say hello to someone on the street, in a café or in a bar and talk. Today people are very suspicious of strangers, and they are right. Experience shows that today many misfortunes have occurred because of meeting bad people.

Nowadays people meet many people through social networks, dating applications, where there are hundreds of thousands of profiles of people looking for friends or a special person to share the rest of their days with.

Although you can never have absolute certainty in these applications, to this day it is the safest thing there is to find friends or that special person we are looking for.

However, we must first make sure before meeting face to face with the person we are talking to, that it is really the person whose profile shows us.

Unfortunately, unpleasant events do happen from time to time, but that should not lead us to the extreme of not wanting to meet people through social networks.

Before contacting a person, we must study well the profile we are interested in. Place of residence, tastes and hobbies. At present, a "hello" is usually enough to start a dialogue, and the initiative can be taken by both men and women, then you can follow up with a question about the city in which you live, and so on.

There is a trick to following a dialogue, because sometimes, after a question is answered, we get stuck, or if we ask too many questions, we end up looking like detectives, and the conversation becomes boring.

It consists of praising something about the person we are talking to, and then asking a question about it. For example.

-How well you keep yourself! Do you go to a gym?

You have well-groomed skin. What kind of creams do you use?

Knowing how to converse is more about knowing how to listen with interest and attention to what the other person says than to what we say, because from what they tell us we can take out one or another topic to continue with the conversation, whether it is written or oral.

Or by asking your opinion about something you have said previously.

And so we can get to know the person with whom we would like to have a date. It is not necessary to rush the first meeting. It is almost certain that the other person also wants to get to know us personally, but sometimes it is good to be a little mysterious/a. There is no need to rush things.

APPROPRIATE CLOTHING

Now let's move on to an aspect that will complement everything we have seen above and will help us gain confidence and self-esteem. It is the clothing. This is a key factor to make a good first impression. We must remember that the first impression is what will remain in the other person's mind when he/she remembers us. This is something psychologically proven.

Young people dress in an informal way. But adults should dress comfortably and formally according to the occasion.

On a first date it is advisable to wear comfortable and elegant clothes, to make a good first impression, later there will be time to wear casual and casual clothes. This goes for both men and women.

The classic jeans for women, with medium or high heel sandals is recommended for a date, and dresses, with colors that can vary according to what you want to project. The classic black, the sensual red, passing through the blue or white tonality that transmits calm and tranquility, or the gray of security.

The clothes for men, it is recommended that they are of dark colors, the classic black or gray tones. Dress shoes are never out of place in a gentleman's presentation. Sportswear is not recommended for a first date.

What is always certain is that elegance in older people, whether men or women, will never go out of fashion, and we will always make a good first impression.

ACCESSORIES

One factor that is always present on the first date, especially in older people, is nerves. As a philosopher said in ancient times: "falling in love at fifteen or doing it at sixty is the same", or, "the nerves on the first time we fall in love or the tenth time it happens to us, are the same", so surely the other person will be just as nervous as we are on the first date.

Accessories are an important complement. For women, a soft perfume and some jewelry, which can even serve as a conversation piece, and for men the same. A cologne or a soft perfume and can be complemented with a watch. And don't forget to bring some mints for this meeting.

AND THE TIME CAME

Let's suppose you have already met a person for a first date. After a nice relaxing bath, the right clothes and a good perfume, what's next?

Choose the right place. A public place is always preferable. It can be a bar, a coffee shop, an outdoor place, a theater. It should be one where you can get an intimate atmosphere and so we can connect with that special person.

It does not necessarily have to be a dinner if it is at night. Some snacks, something to drink and thus eliminate shyness and nerves is ideal, and to be very careful not to overdo it with alcoholic beverages.

There is nothing that scares a person more than getting drunk on the first date, this should be avoided at all costs. A juice or a coffee will never go amiss. Don't rush it.

If all goes well, there will be plenty of time to enjoy that special company. If it is at a different time, coffee, a sandwich and a juice is the most advisable.

THE CONVERSATION

And then came the big moment. They are face to face, face to face, and after the initial greeting and the presentation, it's time to overcome anxiety.

You may be walking in a park, down the street, or sitting in a café or bar. You're both probably nervous. We all have been, and will continue to be, in a similar situation.

The important thing is to be yourself, you should not pretend or lie, because later it will come out in reality what we are, and we will look bad with that person if we do it. There are topics that it is better not to touch on the first date. Religion, politics, soccer. Less about ex-partners.

Remember the trick of praising something about the other person and asking a question about it, and the questions about how to get to know ourselves, which will also help us to get to know other people, and so on. It is also not advisable to talk about yourself.

And in order not to ask so many questions, it is better to know what your opinion is on some topics, such as if you have recently taken a trip, or where you would like to go on vacation.

Let him/her explain as much as possible. And something that should only be used in case of emergency, the cell phone. Don't make the mistake of keeping an eye on it.

There are two things that can scare a person away. Talking about yourself too much, and spending the entire meeting looking at your cell phone.

If the other person is interested, it will certainly help to continue the conversation. To have more topics of conversation sometimes it is necessary to be very detailed. In them you can find topics to continue chatting. And something else. It is not necessary that the first date lasts long. An hour or an hour and a half is enough. It is better to be left with the desire to continue than to bore the other party. That is a risk you run on the first date.

And after the farewell, what comes next?

Let's give it a rest, or as they say, give time to time. We should not rush to go on a second date, nor should we bombard the person with whom we shared the first date with messages or calls.

The next day, both the man and the woman can send a short message thanking her for the company, telling her that she had a great time. Older people tend not to like annoying people very much.

Letting a few days pass before talking again is a good strategy to see if the date went well or not.

Then, either of you can take the first step to engage in conversation and propose a second date. If you both agree, there is an 80% chance that you are at the beginning of a relationship.

But be careful, if the first date was important, the second one is much more important than the first one. This second date could even end up being the beginning of a love relationship, since if one of you did not like the other person, he/she would not agree to go on a second date.

Let's agree at this point that if the first date was a failure, that's no reason to get demoralized.

Repeat the procedure from the beginning until you find the right person to meet for a second date.

We've all been rejected at some point in our lives by someone we were in love with. So it's no big deal if a second date doesn't work out, although statistics show that there is very little chance of this happening.

What's next? An invitation for a second date. If you both agree, the way is clear to go deeper into matters that were not mentioned on the first date, where everything is usually very superficial.

Talking about objectives or goals they have set for the short, medium and long term, personal likes and dislikes, attitudes that bother them, common interests. These are topics about which you can talk for hours and hours.

And how do you know if he really likes you enough to express that to him? You could do it right then or wait for a third date.

Two people who like each other are always looking forward to that moment. If he keeps his eyes on you, pays close attention to what you say, and smiles at the nice things you say about him or her, then it's time to confess that you like him or her.

Who should take this transcendental step: the man or the woman? It doesn't really matter. Either one can do it.

I am of the belief that life has a cycle, everything revolves, and everything returns to the origin following the circle of life. Just as the earth revolves around the sun, and everything is in motion in the universe, fashion returns to what it was fifty years ago, relationships must also fulfill that cycle. And I always bet on chivalry, which will come back sooner or later.

Today, women are very independent, and that has caused men to stop treating them as what they have never ceased to be. Princesses of life, the most beautiful of creation.

Just as flowers perfume, beautify and illuminate nature, women also play this role in life. And who has understood this? We, who have already been through many relationships, who have the necessary experience to realize that. But always, both men and women must support each other to move forward in a relationship.

One alone will not be able to do it without the help of the other. It is not that we do not know these things, but that we often forget them due to the daily hustle and bustle of our existence. We must remember the saying: "Easy come, easy go".

And this is true in all areas and in all things in life. That is why it is not advisable to rush the beginning of a relationship, nor sex. Today, we have sex without commitment, without knowing each other, everything becomes easy, and so relationships do not usually last long. But our intention is to achieve a lasting relationship with the person we choose to accompany until the end.

And when we have already initiated a bond with a person, we have told him/her that we like him/her, that we want to have a relationship, and he/she has responded to our request. What comes next?

THE RELATIONSHIP

Let's suppose that we have already declared our feelings to the person we like, and that we have been reciprocated. Let us remember that if we do not manage to capture the interest of the other person, we go back to the beginning and start again with another one. True love is built little by little. At the beginning, what exists is infatuation, which has a limited duration.

And now comes the most beautiful part of a relationship. The beginning.

The interest in getting to know each other is mutual, and respect is fundamental from the very beginning and throughout life.

It often happens that shortly after the beginning of a love relationship, there is a big fight or argument.

They can even say hurtful words and walk away for a while, and then come back as if nothing had happened, because both people miss each other, and they let that anger pass so as not to discuss any more about what gave rise to the quarrel, but that discussion and the hurtful words that were said, is marked by fire.

This should be avoided at all costs, because the offended person will never forget the event. You can argue, but respect each other. Remember, "Respecting each other", and sincerely apologizing if you have made a mistake.

To make a relationship last, both people must put their all into it. Don't forget that if only one person does everything, love will not last long.

Love is endless between two people who love, care for, respect and admire each other. But it also ends if one or more of those ingredients are missing.

Now we are going to break down this word called "RELATIONSHIP", and look separately at the elements or ingredients that compose it, to try to know more deeply each one of them and to be able to apply the best possible to our own.

COMMUNICATION

Good communication in a couple is one of the fundamental pillars of any relationship. If it fails, the flow of understanding between the two is cut off. Communication is "knowing more about listening than talking".

In many couples, one partner is often less communicative than the other. In cases like this, you have to let her freely give her opinions, complaints or whatever she has to say without interrupting her, so that she is able to express herself with the necessary confidence to be able to communicate what she wants and feels.

By rare coincidence, it usually happens that the other person is more communicative, always wanting to be the dominant party and to be in control of the situation. In such circumstances, the dominant person should never undermine his or her partner, but on the contrary. Help her to be able to express her feelings or any dissatisfaction without feeling pressured by anyone.

If it is the case that both are passive, or its counterpart, both communicative, the best thing to do is to talk calmly and agree on how communication between the two will be more fluid. But the dialogue should never be cut off.

To communicate is to say things without fear or shame, as they say, without mincing words, but never offending, and to clarify together constructively all the doubts you have. This will allow the relationship to consolidate and become stronger every day.

MUTUAL RESPECT

Respect is considered a basic pillar in every relationship. We all like to be respected, so we should reciprocate in the same way, respecting others, but in a couple relationship it is of crucial importance to do so in order to show our spouse how valuable is to us.

Respect means not criticizing, not deciding for her or him, supporting her or his decisions, not trying to override the person we love, letting her or him be authentic/o, and this should be from the very beginning of the relationship, and maintained every day of our lives.

We should also avoid criticizing and speaking ill of his or her parents if he or she has them, or of his or her children if he or she has them from a previous relationship. We must never forget that when we love a person, we accept him or her with what comes with him or her, usually children. We must be understanding and respectful.

We have already said that living with a person is not easy, in fact it is very difficult, but doing things right, has its great rewards. And this goes for both, respect must be mutual, and the slogan: respect and be respected.

We must respect the person we love, their family, as well as their children, and any inconvenience that arises, reach an agreement, talking with our partner. We remind you again that it is important never to speak ill of your family or your children.

Let's respect ourselves, our partner, your children if you have them and your family, and go one step further to have a better relationship.

TRUST THE COUPLE

In reality, all the factors or ingredients that make up a relationship are important. That is why it is difficult to say which are more important and which are less important, when we must talk about each of them, and trust also falls within that range in importance.

Is it possible to have a good relationship if there is no trust in the couple? Let us remember that the intention of this guide is to ensure that people have a good relationship with their partners, and if there is no trust for different reasons, it is impossible to have a good and peaceful coexistence in harmony.

Trust is earned, and one must demonstrate that he/she is a trustworthy person from the beginning. That is why it is important not to lie when two people get to know each other, because over time those lies are discovered and trust is lost. And once lost, it is extremely difficult to regain it.

The person who feels deceived will always question whether what they are being told is true or false. So it is better to save ourselves those future problems and always start a relationship being authentic and truthful in our expressions and feelings.

Trust is never finished. It is like a building, in which every day we place one more brick, called trust, in the structure called relationship.

Let's be trustworthy people for our partners, let's avoid lies and secrets, and let's have a nice relationship.

ACCEPTANCE OF ONESELF AND OF THE COUPLE

We cannot talk about self-acceptance without talking about self-esteem. Both concepts are linked to each other.

To accept oneself is to have the ability to see our defects and virtues, and thus be able to live in peace with ourselves in a conscious way, knowing what we are, and acting accordingly. We talked at the beginning about this topic, and about the questions we could ask ourselves, so that by answering as sincerely as possible, we can get to know ourselves better and accept ourselves as we are.

The most important thing about self-knowledge and self-acceptance is that it gives us the possibility to change in ourselves what we think is wrong, and thus improve and be a better person for ourselves, and most importantly, for our partner.

People who have good self-esteem have better self-acceptance.

It has been proven that in order to love another person better, it is necessary to love oneself first.

How do we do it if we don't love each other enough?

Stop criticizing yourself, be kind and patient with yourself, praise yourself, fill yourself with positive thoughts, indulge in the pleasures you were not giving yourself because of some kind of fear, enjoy each day, we never know when it will be the last one, do not do to others what you would not like them to do to you, be honest with yourself.

Here are some tips to help you love yourself more, so that you will be prepared to love another person well and sincerely.

Now let's move on to acceptance of our partner. Just as knowing ourselves better makes it easier for us to accept ourselves, it also makes it easier for us to accept our partner as he or she is. We should never force ourselves to change anything about him or her if we don't like something. Just as we are not perfect, our partners are not perfect either, and we must respect their way of being. In any case, communication is open to make suggestions, but forcing or forbidding our partner to do something will only create a resentment that will deteriorate our relationship over time. If he/she does not want to change, we must accept him/her or her as he/she is.

And remember something very important. As single adults, we all have a past, and both women and men have children with other people.

Families today are made up of husband, wife, children of the man, children of the woman, and children of the new relationship. And it is essential to accept them all, and treat them as children of the new relationship, to lead a harmonious life together.

There is nothing nicer than living in harmony as a family.

Ladies and gentlemen, let us commit to live in harmony, and to sincerely accept and love ourselves and our partners, and take one more step to strengthen the relationship.

THE FORGIVENESS

Up to this point, we see that all the components of a relationship have the same degree of importance. There is not one for which we can say, this ingredient is not essential in my relationship, and knowing how to forgive is one of them.

There is no perfection in the human being, and for this reason, we all make mistakes, sometimes intentionally, but in most cases involuntarily, when it comes to interacting with a partner. And both components of it must know how to forgive and thus live in harmony.

To forgive is to understand that our partner is a person with faults and virtues, who like us, can make mistakes unintentionally, and it is necessary that we learn to let go of those mistakes and forget them.

We must never tire of remembering that one of the most difficult things in life is to live together well.

And as a philosopher once said, "To leave a relationship to chance or luck is to play Russian roulette".

This is why there are so many people around the world today who separate, because they do not speak clearly and the truthfully from the very beginning of their relationships, and because they leave theirs to chance.

Returning to what concerns us in this part, we must say that forgiveness must be sincere and real, and then forget and never remember again. That means that in future discussions we should not bring up what we have already forgiven.

We should not even think about forgiving, and then take revenge or revenge. If we are going to do that to hurt our partner, it is better to speak well and walk away. Or our relationship will become an endless battlefield, where there will never be a winner.

If both partners learn to forgive each other's mistakes, they will be taking a big step towards a happier life together.

Another very important point to touch on is self-forgiveness. Many times we need to forgive ourselves for mistakes made in the past, which make us live internal conflicts that we do not usually take out of us and we keep a hard battle with our inner self.

One of the ways to solve that is to go to therapy with a psychologist. If we do not have the capacity to go to one, the other way would be to recognize that there are situations that we have gone through in our life, in which we will not be able to go back to fix them.

We must accept that the past cannot be changed, and forgiving ourselves means that we recognize those mistakes, promising not to make them again. And at that moment we must forget and let them go. Doing so will take a weight off our shoulders, as they say, and will help our relationship as a couple to be more harmonious.

LOYALTY AND FIDELITY

We continue with the list of fundamental factors in a relationship, and no less important than the previous ones are loyalty and fidelity.

Loyalty is the respect you have for a person, and is closely linked to fidelity.

Both words together apply to a person who is honest, respectable, who can be believed and trusted, and who will not betray us.

Here we must keep in mind that trust is a basic pillar in the relationship between couples. You have to trust your partner. And it is not possible to have a good relationship when we distrust it.

First of all, we must be loyal and faithful to ourselves, and be aware of the commitment we have made to ourselves.

If two people who love each other, commit to themselves and to each other to be loyal and faithful from the very beginning of their relationship, and remember it all their lives, they will have a wonderful relationship.

If we are not going to be loyal and faithful, it is better to be alone, without harming another person, and thus be able to do what we want, without anyone who can question us and live a quiet life.

But that is not what we want. Most of us human beings are looking for a person who complements us in order to have a dignified and happy life together, and this is achieved by being loyal and faithful as well.

Let's be faithful to our partner and go one step further for a good relationship.

DEMONSTRATION OF LOVE, AFFECTION AND DEAR

Who doesn't like it when your partner talks in your ear saying nice and pleasant things to you, when he/she compliments you, gives you a little gift, tells you that he/she loves you, that he/she loves you and that he/she is happy to have you by his/her side. We all, men and women, like that.

The admiration that a person has for his or her partner is one of the most important ways of showing love.

It is not for nothing that many psychotherapists claim that when a person stops admiring his or her partner, love slowly begins to die.

Poets compare love to a garden full of flowers, which must be watered every day with a little water, without exaggeration, so that the garden remains beautiful and beautiful. And the reality is no less true. The same thing happens in relationships. The love between two people must be watered every day, without exaggeration, with signs of affection, affection, admiration and tenderness.

How do we water it?

With kind words, telling our partner how important he/she is in our life, how much we need him/her, how happy he/she makes us. And to all this we must add kisses and caresses. It is not necessary that they are passionate kisses, that we can leave it for when we have sex, which we will talk about later, but tender, short and soft kisses.

And at this point it is vitally important not to make a very common mistake, which many people have told me about. Especially men. And is that after a while, which can be short or long, the routine makes the couple become very familiar similar to what would be a brother/a. This must be avoided at all costs.

The partner should be loved, cherished, respected, admired, but should always be like an eternal girlfriend or boyfriend, to whom one should always be in the mood for sex. This should never be allowed to die out.

So let's not forget to make presents, however small they may be, such as a flower, a perfume, a piece of jewelry (for women), or a pen, a watch, a glass with his name on it (for men), apart from the demonstrations of affection and love. Tender kisses and words of recognition and admiration to let him/her know that he/she is always in our thoughts, and thus we will take another step towards having a beautiful relationship.

TOLERANCE

Another key ingredient for a good relationship is tolerance. This goes for both partners. Tolerance is basically synonymous with respect. We know that respect is the basis of all human relationships, but in a couple it is much more important because they are the ones with whom you share a lot of time.

Both members of a couple have different characters, different tastes, different customs, and when they start living together, it may happen that they are compatible and it is not an impediment to a good coexistence, or it can also be the most usual. That they are not compatible, and with a good and respectful conversation, they reach an agreement to tolerate those differences.

We see that with good communication all differences between two people can be overcome.

We also notice that all the factors or ingredients that make up a relationship are closely linked and connected to each other.

To be tolerant as a couple, both partners must give their all and apply respect and understanding for a better relationship.

LACK OF INTEREST IN THE COUPLE

"Time inevitably plays havoc with all things," said one philosopher, and that applies to couple relationships as well. No matter how much we fight it, it creeps into our lives and changes us and our surroundings. In almost every relationship, at some point, there is a risk of losing interest in the partner. This is very painful for the person who realizes this, as the other person usually prefers to remain silent.

But let's go to what interests us, and see what could be some reasons that can lead us to lose interest in our partner, so we can be forewarned and know how we can counteract that.

The habit of being together every day and repeating the same activities can lead us to lose interest in our relationship.

Falling in love with a person is one of the most sublime and beautiful feelings of human beings. When we fall in love, everything changes within us. From our mood, to our mental and emotional state, including our state of health.

As time goes by, this infatuation gives way to what is called "companionate love", where habit makes us feel secure of our couple and it does not cross our minds that we may lose him/her. In other words, we let ourselves be, and for many people, this lack of interest is normal.

But that is not true, it is not normal, and as soon as one realizes that, it must be discussed as a couple. Here we must remember that both parties are committed to make every effort to move the relationship forward, and the doors of communication should always be open to solve together any problems that may arise.

If after talking it over, the problem is not solved, the best thing to do is to turn to a couple's therapist. Do not skimp on resources to try to regain interest in the person you love.

If you are both aware of the importance of maintaining interest in your partner, and try to work it out together if it should arise, you will be one step closer to having a good relations.

FRIENDSHIP IN THE COUPLE

"For a good relationship, your best friend, must be your partner". It's a saying that's not entirely true. It doesn't have to be.

If it happens, welcome it. It is one of the most beautiful feelings that exist, and in a couple it makes the relationship more lasting, harmonious and fun.

We know that friendship must be worked on, cared for and respected, and in a couple we can achieve this by dedicating special time to share together, as we do with friends.

Telling each other all the things that happen and showing interest in what they tell us is a way to be very good friends.

Plan a vacation together, have a spontaneous date, such as a snack or dinner somewhere romantic, laugh together, choose a movie that you both like and watch at night sitting next to each other, or if you have children, when they are not there or have gone to sleep. Practice sports together, go out on a weekend alone, without the children, if there are any. Be reliable and give good advice.

By sharing some of these activities together, and sometimes with other friends, you will become good friends and the relationship will be strengthened.

GOOD HUMOR IN THE COUPLE

Having a good sense of humor in the couple, as well as a good friendship, will strengthen the bond of love that unites them and create a stable and lasting relationship.

Never allow bad moods to dominate your life, nor make you go to bed angry. The causes of anger should be resolved before going to bed.

In the stage of falling in love between two people, they are covered by such a great energy of happiness, love, and good humor, that without effort the relationship is wonderful. That is a key moment, so that if we realize, and we want our relationship to continue at that level, we must do everything possible to keep it the same by being tolerant, loyal, communicative, respectful, romantic. And to all of that always add a pinch of good humor.

Life should not be taken too seriously, there are situations over which we will never be able to have control. But everything is more bearable, with a little humor at least. Laughing is healthy, and if you do it as a couple, it's great.

A couple that loves each other, where there is good communication, respect, loyalty, empathy, good sex and a good sense of humor is indestructible. An expert in couples says. Two people who love each other and have a good sense of humor will always be happy.

And it has been proven to be so.

Smiling often is the beginning of having a good sense of humor. Seeing the funny side of many everyday situations is also a good way to have a good sense of humor.

Science says that when you laugh, your body releases the happiness hormones: dopamine, serotonin and endorphin.

When a person has an orgasm, the body releases those same happiness hormones. That's why we feel just as good after laughing a lot or having an orgasm.

How about we start smiling more in our daily lives and at our partner, and take another step towards a wonderful relationship?

EMPATHY

We come to another of the essential factors or ingredients to have a good relationship. But let's first see what empathy is.

Empathy is the ability of a person to put him/herself in the place of another person, and from that point of view to understand the feelings and emotions that person is going through in a given situation.

Now let's focus on empathy between two people who love each other.

We repeat, it is one of the pillars of a good relationship. Without empathy, many relationships have ended shortly after living together. Empathy and respect go hand in hand.

Lack of understanding in a couple is synonymous with lack of empathy.

According to therapists, the greater the empathy, the greater the sexual satisfaction.

If one or both partners lack empathy, they should go to couples therapy. It is the most advisable thing to do, because you can learn to be empathic and thus save the relationship.

All couples go through times of conflict, and in those moments it is important to be empathetic. Settle those conflicts in peace, without arguing, with a lot of patience and understanding on the part of both partners, respecting opinions and not judging.

Thousands of couples who have attended therapy have saved their relationship by learning empathy.

Let us always understand our partner with empathy, and support her. Let's be more empathetic with her, and if we can't be, let's go to therapy to learn it, and let's make our relationship a wonderful experience.

WORKING ON THE RELATIONSHIP

When we talk about working on the relationship, we are not referring to doing it when we are going through a crisis in the couple, but as a prevention to avoid that in the near future something serious could happen that could lead to a crisis without a solution.

It is better to know first some factors that could lead us to make our relationship fail, and then see what we can do to avoid it.

So let's first see what are some of those factors that can put our relationship at risk.

-Not allowing time to share in intimacy, and by "intimacy", we do not only refer to what has to do with sex, but to sharing a romantic dinner, a walk holding hands, going to the movies, an activity where just the two of you are alone.

-Trying to change our partner when we don't like something about him or her. A saying about relationships goes: "If you don't like something about your partner, you should change yourself". And never better said for these cases. We must respect our spouse and accept him or her as he or she is. Many problems in couples start when one of the partners wants to change the other. Let's not make that mistake.

-Resentment or resentment. This is one of the worst feelings that exist. It makes us move away from our partner, and our partner move away from us. Resentment is a deep anger or anger due to a harm that has been done to us, and that settles inside us for a long time, and in that state we do not allow the person against whom it is directed to approach us, and in the long run, that person gets farther and farther away. The consequences are constant fights and arguments.

-Being selfish. If we love our partner, we must help him/her to grow, be sincere and be interested in his/her personal growth as well as in our own.

The selfish person only wants to grow and does not care about the needs of his or her spouse.

-Pride. This is a feeling that if not controlled can seriously affect the love relationship between two people. It is related to self-esteem. The proud person, whether male or female, is an insecure person, with low self-esteem, and to protect himself, he makes use of this destructive feeling.

These feelings that we have mentioned, can together or on their own, destroy a relationship. How can we overcome them so that they do not jeopardize ours, since at some point in our coexistence they can affect us, since we are not immune to any of them.

Share some time with our partner. If there are children, set aside one day a week for a romantic outing. If there are no children, a whole weekend for just the two of you. Men can send a bouquet of flowers or a box of chocolates from time to time. Men like to receive a romantic message from our partners or something related to a sexual encounter.

Be open to dialogue permanently, talk about different topics, without trying to change their way of being, and solving any kind of anger or tantrum before going to bed, putting both parties in search of a solution to the conflict that arises.

Selfishness and pride are two feelings that go hand in hand and are closely linked.

Most people do not want to acknowledge that they are selfish and proud, whether they are men or women.

If you really care about your partner and the relationship, you must make an effort to realize that these feelings are part of you. Generally other people often tell us that we are, and we tend to deny, but when it comes to our relationship we should not let it go unnoticed, and realizing that, we should follow some tips that experts give us to change and improve. Our partner will notice the change, because it is very noticeable when a selfish and proud person stops being selfish and proud, and will be very grateful for it.

Let's start by accepting that not always the reason will be on our side, that the important thing is not to be superior to other people, but the essential thing is to surpass yourself every day. Listen more to your partner and put yourself in his or her shoes practicing empathy.

A law of the universe says: "You get what you give", so let's start to selflessly help other people, and with more reason to our partner, you will see that over time you will be rewarded.

Love your partner, take care of them, and work on your relationship for a wonderful life.

SOBERBIA AND PROUD

This feeling is one of the most destructive in a couple. Arrogant people, men or women, believe they are the center of the universe, do not accept criticism, are contemptuous and only seek to be admired through their presence and intelligence. They try to humiliate their partners and lack empathy.

They only talk about themselves, their plans and goals and never listen to their couples.

It is very difficult to live with an arrogant person, because they are almost always giving orders and waiting for them to obey with submission what they ask for.

What can we do if our partner is an arrogant person, or if we are arrogant ourselves?

As we said at the beginning, a visit to a psychologist from time to time can help to solve many problems, because the arrogant person does not want to recognize that he/she is arrogant, and almost never does.

That is why we should try to convince to go together to a couple therapy if our spouse does not want to change, because with that attitude the relationship can end, although those people never want that, but they do not realize the damage they cause in the other person.

Only with a specialist can you try to change the proud couple.

What happens if we are arrogant and want to change to save our love bond, but we cannot go for some reason to a therapist?

Then we must look at our relationship objectively, from a different point of view than our own, as if the problem were with a friendly couple, and we would like to give him or her advice.

There we will realize the situation we are going through, and we will have to make some changes in our behavior if we want to keep a good relationship and our partner.

We must admit that we are not perfect, that we can make mistakes like everyone else, we must respect other people as we would like to be respected, we must recognize that despite being intelligent, we can learn from other people, and we must stop teasing and humiliating our partner and other people.

This way we can change and lead a better life with our spouse for a better relationship.

JEALOUSY

This ingredient should be in the top three of the list due to its importance.

Who has not felt jealousy at least once in his life? Jealousy is a very destructive feeling. How many crimes have been committed in its name? This feeling blinds and can drive anyone to madness.

Jealousy in the couple, means suspicion, fear, insecurity in the loved one, and in oneself, fear of losing it.

There are common or normal jealousies, which we all have at times, when we feel our partner is far away from us, emotionally or in our feelings.

There is also unhealthy jealousy, and that is very dangerous.

The pathologically jealous person does not trust his or her partner, wants to possess him or her exclusively, controls him or her day and night, where he or she goes, who he or she talks to, checks his or her cell phone and social networks. They do not mind not doing their work or fulfilling all their obligations, as long as they know what their partner is doing while they are not with him or her.

They may even use violence when they are not satisfied with the explanations they receive.

Generally, the jealous person is also violent.

In most cases, relationships end badly or with misfortune. Today it is advisable to get away as soon as possible from a person who is sick with jealousy.

But, what to do to overcome jealousy in oneself, or if the partner is jealous?

The best thing to do is to go to a professional in couples therapy, where you will surely improve a lot and you will be able to rebuild your relationship normally.

If you do not have the means to do so, there are some tips that can help you. The best thing to do is for both partners to talk it over and help each other.

Do not forget that you should always leave the way of communication open.

First of all, it is necessary to recognize that one suffers from this evil called unhealthy jealousy.

Then it is important to work together with the partner to affirm the self-esteem of the jealous person.

The latter should know that with her jealousy, she could lose the loved one if she persists in keeping this feeling.

The jealous person should not look into his or her partner's social networks, and for a reasonable time, neither should he or she look into his or her own until he or she overcomes the problem that afflicts him or her. The jealous person is usually obsessed with imaginary situations that have not yet occurred, and that are only in his or her mind.

They have in their favor, that this mental disorder called jealousy can be cured.

Those who suffer from unhealthy jealousy should reaffirm their self-esteem, trust their partner, and try to lead a normal relationship, and the partner can help by giving them reasons to change and making them realize how important they are to you. Overcome jealousy together by talking and trusting each other, and take a step towards a better relationship.

ROMANTICISM AND DETAILS

Who doesn't like to have a romantic and detail-oriented person by their side. Both men and women, if they had to choose, would choose such a person.

By nature, women are more detail-oriented and romantic than men, but that does not mean that men are not.

At the beginning of a relationship, men are usually very detailed, in the sense of giving gifts and tokens of romanticism to the loved one, but as time goes by, these details tend to become more and more spaced out, until after several years, in most cases, they remain in the memory. On the other hand, women tend to always be detail-oriented despite the passage of time. By their very nature, it is easier for them to be so. They remember birthdays, anniversaries, and never forget to give a present to their partner or friends.

After a few years, men find it harder to be men, and a little trick to not forget to be romantic, to remember birthdays and anniversaries, is to put a note in a drawer or in the reminder part of the cell phone.

We should never forget our partner's birthday, wedding anniversary, or even the date and day you met. With any small gift, be it a flower or a box of chocolates, we will look like princes.

Our partner must always have priority in our relationship. Let's give it the importance it deserves. It is another very important detail for a good relationship.

I want to re-emphasize a point that some people have brought to my attention.

I have been asked when reading this guide, what happened if a person was not detail or romantic, or not jealous at all, or just didn't want to be, and I told them that this book is aimed at people who really want to do something different and good in their lives with respect to their partners. If they do not have those intentions, today they can perfectly well opt for solitude, or to live each one in their respective homes, having a dating relationship. Perfectly understandable, being an interesting alternative as well.

We know that thousands of books have been written on the subject of couples and relationships, this being one more of them, and although it has nothing new, I hope it will help you to remember many things that we know, but we forget to apply when the time comes to do it with the person we love and who is next to us.

Let's be sincerely detailed and romantic with our partner, and let's take another step towards having a beautiful relationship.

THE MONEY

Is it difficult to talk about money in a couple?

Yes, it is, and very much so, but you should not be afraid to do so, and the sooner you talk about the economic issue in a relationship and establish some simple rules the better, so you will avoid future headaches.

Of course, money problems do not happen in all couples, but in most of them they do, and there are even breakups due to misunderstandings in money management.

There is no better solution than to keep the communication channel open to talk as clearly as possible and reach an agreement on the economic issue, because in many relationships people do not want to mention the subject of personal expenses, common expenses, credit cards and savings.

It is key to set goals on how to spend the money, and what the money saved will be used for. For travel, to buy a property, or to invest in a business.

You should consider the money in common, and also the personal money of each one. And above all, respect the opinions of both parties.

It may be the case that both are savers, or that one is and the other is not.

In both situations it is good to talk without getting into serious arguments, which often happens. And it is not a big deal. If that happens, you should agree to leave the conversation for another day. The important thing is to reach an agreement that benefits both parties, or that both give something up.

It is good that you make a family budget and talk about retirement if there is one.

Talk about money, come to an agreement that benefits both of you, put your love for your partner above money, and take another step towards a happy cohabitation.

ADMIRATION FOR THE COUPLE

When a relationship begins, two feelings appear. The first is infatuation, and the second is admiration for the person. After a while, which is usually a little less than a year, the infatuation disappears to give way to love, which is maintained with the help of admiration.

Admiring the person we love is very important to keep the flame of love burning. We can ask ourselves: What are the things we like about our partner?

And the answer to that question is what we admire in that person. But it must be something personal, internal to her, not external, because the external may end at some point, and therefore there would be nothing left to admire in her if she no longer existed. And what we admire internally is what attracts us to her.

But what if after a while that person changes, and we no longer have anything to admire? Here many people begin to wonder: why stay together?

It is therefore important to communicate to the person of the internal qualities that one admires in him/her, so that he/she can notice and reinforce if possible. The admired person, in gratitude for the recognition of his virtues, will tend to continue to do the same, and will return that gratitude, admiring his partner as well.

And let's remember once again that a relationship is made by two people, both must put a lot of effort to carry out the bond that unites them. If only one of them is the one who does everything in the relationship, it is doomed to failure, or to lead a life together full of frustrations.

Both of you should ask yourselves: What do I admire in my partner?

Then, kindly tell each other what you admire about each other, and more importantly. Improve sincerely in order to continue to be admired.

Let us sincerely admire the person next to us, let us communicate what we admire about him or her, and let us go one step further to have a wonderful life.

DEPRESSION

Here we are going to touch on depression in the couple in a superficial way. Knowing that the best way to treat it is to consult a medical professional.

Depression is classified as a mental disorder produced by a change or a great loss in a person, such as a serious illness, loss of a close relative, or loss of a job among many other reasons, and produces in the affected person, changes in mood, and a great sadness.

Many times, at the beginning it is usually confused with a bad mood when the causes are not well known. But with the passing of days or weeks, and when no improvement is seen, the person is diagnosed with advanced depression.

How can we realize if our partner, or we ourselves are in a depressive state?

If we notice any of these symptoms in ourselves or in our partner, it is imperative to see a doctor, a psychologist or a psychiatrist as soon as possible.

-Attacks of anger, bad mood or irritability on a constant basis.

-A lot of tiredness, fatigue and lack of appetite for several days.

-Being sad, melancholic and lack of concentration.

-Easy crying for no apparent reason.

-Feeling pessimistic and hopeless for a long time.

How can we help the specialist, or if it is something minor and we cannot consult for some reason?

-Good nutrition, as healthy as possible.

-Daily physical activity.

-Discuss the problems that afflict the depressed person with someone he or she trusts who is a good listener. Sometimes it is good to unburden oneself to a responsible person.

-Try to think positive thoughts.

-Filling time with healthy activities such as reading, listening to music, taking a course on crafts to prevent stress.

Taking care of our mental health and that of our partner, and supporting each other in good times and bad will make us take another fundamental step towards a better relationship.

SEX

Sex is one of the most interesting topics for people of all ages, but here we will focus superficially on sex in adults.

What can we say about sex to begin with?

That we should enjoy it to the fullest, and get out of our minds all those preconceived ideas and thoughts that we might have read or heard somewhere.

First of all, let's say that when two people meet and fall in love, they seek sex as a form of bonding that brings them closer together. But in adult people it is advisable to wait until a third or fourth date to do it.

There is a saying: "Easy come, easy go". Young people who live a very accelerated life, the first thing they look for is sex, and so most relationships do not last long.

But if what we are looking for is a lasting relationship, it is better to know a little more about the person with whom we share before having responsible sex. By responsible, we mean taking care of ourselves, both men and women, to avoid sexually transmitted infections.

DEMYSTIFYING MYTHS

We have been told so much about the loss of virility, about sexual frequency in older people, about relationships between young and old people, about the loss of sexual desire, about menopause and other factors, as to make us afraid of sex in adulthood, and in most cases, all these factors are nothing more than myths.

They say that sexual frequency in older people is drastically reduced, that they have an average of once a week, four times a month. However, many studies have been done around the world on the sexual frequency that couples have, and it turns out that these studies show that couples in their thirties to fifties have a sexual frequency of four to five times a month after the first year. Almost the same ratio as in older people.

Science has also demystified the myth of menopause and post menopause in women. Today there are many accessible medical treatments so that women can enjoy sex in these two stages of their lives, without complications, with more freedom, and enjoying sexual relations to the fullest.

It will always be very important to visit a specialist to ensure good sexual health.

Much has been said and written about the loss of virility in men, but doctors today claim that there are many methods to return, if not one hundred percent, at least eighty percent of virility to older people, which is enough to have a good sexual relationship.

Let us remember that sex, in both women and men, begins in the brain, in the mind, and from there they control the genitals.

According to sex therapists, ninety-five percent of sexual desire in people, both men and women, is a product of the sexual thoughts a person has, and the remaining five percent depends on the sensations felt in the body.

So we see that for a good sexual intercourse, the key is to relax, leave the nerves aside, talking or having a drink to relax the atmosphere in the couple, having sexual thoughts, which will produce the excitement, and when complemented with caresses and sexual games, will produce the erection of the penis and lubrication in the vagina of the woman for a good intercourse.

Having good sex is about both partners enjoying the sexual act. And to the question, what is allowed and what is not allowed in sex? The answer given by sexologists is that in sex between adults, everything that both partners agree on is allowed.

Both should put all their desire to excite each other. In youth, foreplay is often overlooked, but in adults it is very necessary to do it, calm and relaxed.

For this, in the preliminaries, as it is called to those foreplay before sex, you can watch together a movie with explicit sex scenes, read or watch erotic magazines, use sex toys, massage and caress each other, even masturbation as a couple is recommended by sexologists.

Everything you agree on as a couple is valid in foreplay. If there is something that bothers you, it is better to leave it alone. No one should be forced to do something they don't like in the sexual encounter.

Another important complement for sexual encounters is food. Sexuality experts recommend foods that help the body produce serotonin, which they call the hormone of happiness, and those that increase blood circulation. These foods are recommended for both men and women.

-Dark chocolate.

-Strawberries.

-Nutmeg.

-Avocado.

-Oysters.

-Cinnamon.

-Garlic.

-Ginger.

-watermelon.

A doctor said: Nowadays there are no more excuses to have good sex. If something else is missing, there are pills with sildenafil, better known as Viagra, which produce wonderful effects on men's erection, of course, after a medical check-up.

There have even been medical studies with women, where sildenafil produces positive effects in women with problems of decreased libido.

Another topic that many people question is the relationship between young people and adults.

Nowadays it is normal to see couples with many years difference in their ages. There is nothing wrong with that. What could be questioned is the future of the relationship if that difference is too pronounced. But if two adult people agree to have a relationship despite the age disparity, no one should object if they are aware and have a common feeling.

Youth can be perfectly complemented with experience.

A couple should give each other love, admiration, respect and have good sexual moments for an excellent relationship.

We have already seen a good number of factors or ingredients that influence a couple's relationship in order to make it bearable and harmonious.

Surely we all know these factors, but in almost all relationships we forget to apply them after a while, more because of the daily grind.

That is why it is important to remember them from time to time, and one of the tricks to do this is to write on one or several pieces of paper, and paste on the inside of our closet door or behind the bathroom mirror where the toiletries are kept, or in some other place we frequent in our home, a reminder that reminds us every day, how to treat our partner with love, respect and affection.

And always knowing that this goes for both partners. We will never tire of repeating that a couple relationship is made by two people. It is not enough for one to give everything and the other nothing. If this happens, the end result will be a life full of sadness and unhappiness, or a breakup.

When we speak of love, respect and affection, we are also referring to the fact that all forms of violence, whether verbal, psychological or physical, have no place in a relationship. We should not accept a violent person in our relationship.

If we realize that we have a violent person in our life, the best thing to do is to get away from them as soon as possible before we get used to suffering at their side. Life is to be happy, not to suffer. Another option is to go to couple's therapy so that the violent person changes his or her attitude if he or she really loves his or her spouse.

Now I am going to transcribe a fable, so that after reading it, you can analyze the moral of the story.

Once upon a time in the history of the world, there was a terrible day when Hate, who is the king of bad feelings, defects and bad virtues, summoned to an urgent meeting all the black feelings of the world and the most perverse desires of the human heart. They came to the meeting curious to know what the purpose was. When they were all there, Hatred spoke and said:

-I have gathered you all here because I want to kill someone with all my strength.

The attendees were not very surprised, for it was the Hate talking, and he always wants to kill someone, yet they all wondered among themselves who would be so hard to kill that Hate needed them all.

-I want Love to be killed," he said. Many smiled malevolently, because more than one wanted to destroy it.

The first volunteer was Bad Character, who said:

-I will do it, and I assure you that in a year Love will be dead; I will provoke such discord and rage that it will not bear it.

At the end of a year they met again, and on hearing the report of the Bad Character they were disappointed.

-I'm sorry, I tried everything, but every time I sowed discord, Love overcame it and came out ahead.

It was then that, very diligently, Ambition offered herself, who flaunting her power said:

-Since Bad Character has failed, I will go. I will divert Love's attention to the desire for wealth and power. That will never ignore him.

And Ambition began its attack on its victim, who was indeed wounded but, after struggling to get out of it, gave up all desire for power and triumphed again.

Hate, furious at the failure of Ambition, sent Jealousy, who mockingly and perversely invented all sorts of tricks and situations to mislead Love and hurt him with doubts and unfounded suspicions. But the confused Love wept and thought that he did not want to die, and with courage and fortitude he overcame them, and defeated them.

Year after year, Hatred continued in its struggle sending its most hurtful companions, it sent Coldness, Selfishness, Cantankerousness, Indifference, Poverty, Disease and many others who always failed, because when Love felt faint it took strength again and overcame everything.

Hate, convinced that Love was invincible, said to the others: - "There is nothing to be done. Love has endured everything, we have been insisting for many years and we have not succeeded".

Suddenly, in a corner of the room, someone unrecognizable stood up, dressed all in black and wearing a giant hat that fell over his face and did not let him be seen, his appearance was funereal like that of death.

-I will kill Love," he said confidently. They all wondered who it was that pretended to do alone what none had been able to do. Hate said:

- "Go and do it."

Only some time had passed when Hate called back all the bad feelings to tell them that after much waiting, Love HAD finally DIED. All were happy, but surprised.

Then the feeling in the black hat spoke:

-There I deliver Love to you totally dead and shattered," and without another word he left.

- "Wait," said Hate, "in so short a time you wiped him out completely, you made him desperate and he made not the slightest effort to live. Who are you?"

The feeling lifted for the first time its hideous face and said,

"I am The Routine."

THE TEACHING: Routine is a feeling that can destroy and kill a relationship.

Habit, repetitive acts, silences for days, boredom, inevitably lead to routine, and although that happens in almost ninety-nine percent of couples at some point, it is what must be overcome to move forward.

Nowadays there are many activities that can be done as a couple to break the monotony and routine, and always, agreeing to talk is essential.

Practice together some sporting activity such as walking, swimming, going to the gym, listening to music, reading books, going to the movies, going for a walk, having a coffee or a drink in a bar, watching a series or movie together, taking a course, writing poems, stories or novels.

Maybe you have the talent to write and you don't dare to take it out of you. With a little imagination you will find other activities to break the routine in your lives and in sex. Don't forget that talking, conversing and giving your opinion to each other will enrich your relationship.

If you are one of those people who like to be connected to social networks, on the computer or with the cell phone, which is not recommended for a long time, because they are generators of jealousy, distrust and insecurities in the relationship, it is better to talk and reach an agreement on the time in which you will remain connected, and thus, be bored together each in their own world (sarcasm).

Being bored alone, having your partner next to you doing some idle activity, such as being on social networks, makes you wonder many times what you are doing there alone. On the other hand, two people sharing bored time having some similar activity, as in the example above, one next to the other with their respective mobiles connected to the internet for a pre-established time, will make the routine more bearable.

In conclusion, we will say that in this guide you may not find anything new, because we all know about love, sex, and the main factors involved in them, and we think we know how to solve them when problems arise. Especially the young people who almost never listen to us, but experience tells us that at the time of applying them, almost nobody remembers them, and what we seek here is to refresh their memory so that they do not forget that if they want to have a relationship until the end of their days, they must sincerely love their partners, and both must put the best they have for it.

Nobody said it would be easy, and just as we take care of our vehicle, giving it a shower every weekend, or sending it somewhere to have it done, so that it is always presentable, taking it to the workshop when it presents a problem, or as we take care of our computers, our work or business, in the same way we must take care of our relationship, even more, because it is the engine that moves our lives, and that can give us joys and happiness if we take care of it, or unhappiness and sadness if we do not.

Let's love our partner, let's talk to her, let's respect her opinion, let's have her present at all times, let's have empathy towards her, let's leave aside pride, anger and resentment, let's accept her as she is and have confidence in her, let's give her love, affection and good sex, let's laugh and have fun together, let's be accomplices, let's leave infidelities, criticisms and pride aside, let's set goals together for the week, the month, the year, let's really admire her and let's talk about money without any kind of shame.

Let's spend more time with our spouse than with our cell phone, computer and social networks, and let's find ways to eliminate routine from our lives by using our imagination.

Let's write down on a piece of paper the tips that seem most important to us, and put them in a place that is visible to us, to remember them from time to time, so we never forget them, neither birthdays, nor anniversaries, and let's be the happiest people with our partners in healthy and wonderful relationships.

And as a corollary to all this, let's say that most older people who want to rebuild their lives, living together again with their loved one, do not necessarily need to remarry. This would be one more option for couples to opt for.

Life is very beautiful, and as a couple, with a person with whom we get along well, it is wonderful.

Life is to enjoy and be happy as a couple, not to have a life of misfortunes and suffer next to one person.

And both must put all of themselves to achieve it.

If this self-help guide can change one couple's life for the better, it will have done its job.

END